आ नो भद्राः क्रतवो यन्तु विश्वतः

Let noble thoughts come to us from every side

—**Rigveda, I-89-i**

BHAVAN'S BOOK UNIVERSITY

192

UPANISHADS

by

C. RAJAGOPALACHARI

BOOKS BY

C. RAJAGOPALACHARI

PUBLISHED BY THE BHAVAN

Ramayana

Mahabharata

Rajaji's Speeches Vol. I

Rajaji's Speeches Vol. II

Hinduism: Doctrine and Way of Life

Bhagavad Gita

Stories for the Innocent

Kural — The Great Book of Tiru-Valluvar

Upanishads

Our Culture

Bhaja Govindam

Gandhiji's Teachings & Philosophy

Avvaiar (The Great Tamil Poet)

Kathopanishad (Tamil)

Rescue Democracy From Money Power

Bhagavad Gita (Hindi)

Upanishads (Hindi-Cum-English Edition)

Bhajagovind (Kannada)

BHAVAN'S BOOK UNIVERSITY

UPANISHADS

C. RAJAGOPALACHARI

2024

BHARATIYA VIDYA BHAVAN
Kulapati K. M. Munshi Marg
Mumbai - 400007

First Edition : 1963
Second Edition : 1966
Third Edition : 1973
Fourth Edition : 1982
Fifth Edition : 1989
Sixth Edition : 1991
Seventh Edition : 1996
Eighth Edition : 2007
Ninth Edition : 2011
Tenth Edition : 2016
Eleventh Edition : 2021
Twelfth Edition : 2024

Price : ₹ 115/-

PRINTED IN INDIA

By Atul Goradia at Siddhi Printers, 13/14, Bhabha Building,
13th Khetwadi Lane, Mumbai - 400004, and
Published by P. V. Sankarankutty Director
for the Bharatiya Vidya Bhavan,
Kulapati Munshi Marg, Mumbai - 400007.
E-mail : publications@bhavans.info
Web-site : www.bhavans.info

KULAPATI'S PREFACE

The Bharatiya Vidya Bhavan—that Institute of Indian Culture in Bombay—needed a Book University, a series of books which, if read, would serve the purpose of providing higher education. Particular emphasis, however, was to be put on such literature as revealed the deeper impulsions of India. As a first step, it was decided to bring out in English 100 books, 50 of which were to be taken in hand almost at once. Each book was to contain from 200 to 250 pages.

It is our intention to publish the books we select, not only in English, but also in the following Indian languages: Hindi, Bengali, Gujarati, Marathi, Tamil, Telugu, Kannada and Malayalam.

This scheme, involving the publication of 900 volumes, requires ample funds and an all-India organisation. The Bhavan is exerting its utmost to supply them.

The objectives for which the Bhavan stands are the re-integration of Indian culture in the light of modern knowledge and to suit our present-day needs and the resuscitation of its fundamental values in their pristine vigour.

Let me make our goal more explicit:

We seek the dignity of man, which necessarily implies the creation of social conditions which would allow him freedom to evolve along the lines of his own temperament and capacities; we seek the harmony of individual efforts and social relations, not in any makeshift way, but within the frame-work of the Moral Order; we seek the creative art of life, by the alchemy of which human limitations are progressively transmuted, so that man may become the instrument of God, and is able to see Him in all and all in Him.

The world, we feel, is too much with us. Nothing would uplift or inspire us so much as the beauty and aspiration which such books can teach. In this series, therefore, the literature of India, ancient and modern, will be published in a form easily accessible to all. Books in other literatures of the world, if they illustrate the principles we stand for, will also be included.

This common pool of literature, it is hoped, will enable the reader, eastern or western, to understand and appreciate currents of world thought, as also the movements of the mind in India, which, though they flow through different linguistic channels, have a common urge and aspiration.

Fittingly, the Book University's first venture is the *Mahabharata*, summarised by one of the greatest living Indians, C. Rajagopalachari; the second work is on a section of it, the *Gita* by H. V. Divatia, an eminent jurist and a student of philosophy. Centuries ago, it was proclaimed of the *Mahabharata*: "What is not in it, is nowhere." After twenty-five centuries, we can use the same words about it. He who knows it not, knows not the heights and depths of the soul; he misses the trials and tragedy and the beauty and grandeur of life.

The *Mahabharata* is not a mere epic; it is a romance, telling the tale of heroic men and women and of some who were divine; it is a whole literature in itself, containing a code of life; a philosophy of social and ethical relations, and speculative thought on human problems that is hard to rival; but, above all, it has for its core the *Gita*, which is, as the world is beginning to find out, the noblest of scriptures and the grandest of sagas in which the climax is reached in the wondrous Apocalypse in the Eleventh Canto.

Through such books alone the harmonies underlying true culture, I am convinced, will one day reconcile the disorders of modern life.

I thank all those who have helped to make this new branch of the Bhavan's activity successful.

K. M. Munshi

INTRODUCTION

In the *Upanishads,* we have a scripture which, among all the holy scriptures of the world, displays the most scientific spirit in connection with spiritual enquiry. The sages, whose thoughts and teachings we read in the *Upanishads,* seem to be as much inspired by constructive doubt as the most modern men of science. Their questions and answers indicate that they lived in an age when, alongside of conformism and the rigid maintenance of old practices, men thirsted for Truth and the atmosphere was charged with the boldest freethought: *Satyamevajayate nanrtam satyenapantha vitato devayanah.*

The conformism that prevails in our own midst today, in spite of so much science and freethought, does not confuse us. We are familiar with it and we find no difficulty in appraising and evaluating in their true measure both the conflicting elements, orthodox practice as well as the prevailing scepticism. But the conformism of some thousands of years ago is a very different thing. We understand it much less, if at all, and it, therefore, blurs the picture. We may fail for this reason rightly to appreciate the spirit of enquiry which dominated the mind and lives of the sages whose teachings are recorded in the *Upanishads*, and which is reflected in every line of this great scripture of India.

If we learn to make due allowance for the time-interval, and have enlightenment and elasticity of mind enough to be able to use and profit by a holy book with invaluable hoary associations, without having to get the text actually expurgated and revised in order to exclude the irrelevancies and the mere background of a bygone age, we cannot have a better book of religion for modern times than the *Upanishads*. The spacious imagination, the majestic sweep of thought and the almost reckless spirit of exploration with which, urged by the compelling thirst for Truth, the *Upanishad* teachers and pupils dig into the Open Secret of the Universe, make this most ancient among the world's holy books still the most modern and most satisfying.

It is probable that the *Upanishads* were originally composed somewhat as notes of lectures, intended to assist the pupil's memory in subsequent reflection. They were not composed as text-books of philosophy to serve by themselves, as books are now written. Notes in our days would be short indicative phrases written to dictation or taken down by the students themselves. But, in the old days, they took the shape of verses to be memorized, as writing played a lesser part in learning than it does now. Placed before us today in the shape of printed matter, with title-page, contents and index all complete, the *Upanishads* perplex us in many places with their seeming simplicity of language, covering thoughts that are far from clear. Isolated from teacher and without personal expansion and explanation, these compositions confuse us with antithesis and epigram and the use of the same word in varying senses, a style which we should have particularly avoided when discussing difficult problems. All this is, however, understandable if we remember that they were not books to displace teacher but were notes to standardize teaching and to help memory.

Apart from the difficulty arising out of the form, and the difference of purpose of the composition from that of modern books, the distance that divides us from the day when these thoughts were propounded makes the greatest difficulty. The reflections were necessarily hung on to the life, beliefs and manners of those ancient times. To understand the meaning and the point of what was said by men of a long past age, we have to get back to the circumstances of that age, a task of great difficulty even for the most imaginative among us.

Beliefs and practices that are to us obviously childish formed the large and main background of life in those days, and the reflections of the best and wisest men of those days, which necessarily referred to and were set on the background of their own daily life, have to be interpreted by us, eliminating that background. What was very real and serious to them is to us childish, untenable and of no consequence, so that even the reflections thereon become un-understandable. The process of seeing a picture apart from the background is not easy. We are apt to lose ourselves in the reactions produced in our modern minds by the beliefs and practices referred to, and fail to grasp the essential amidst the distractions of the incidental.

In studying the *Upanishads*, we come against repeated references to ceremonials, sacrifices and the worship of gods and discussions as to their efficacy, which confuse the deeper and predominant enquiry. The position becomes to the Hindu readers worse still on account of the formal persistence in Hinduism even now of the shell of those beliefs and practices. To interpret and evaluate the substance of the *Upanishads*, we need a powerful imagination and an intellectual elasticity that can jump over the tremendous space that divides the beliefs, aspirations and psychologies of modern life from those of a long-past age. A study of the full text of the longer *Upanishads* would be the best means of comprehending the mind of the fathers of Hinduism. But at the same time, the difficulties pointed out above reach the greatest dimensions in these longer *Upanishads*. In making the selections for the following chapters, an attempt has been made to reduce these difficulties to the minimum without prejudice to the main purpose of presenting an adequate idea of the *Upanishad*-content.

CONTENTS

KATHOPANISHAD

EVERY Hindu knows the great Kurukshetra scene, which forms the prologue of the *Bhagavad Gita*—the warrior, stricken by remorse and doubt, throwing himself at the mercy of his divine charioteer for guidance. The *Katha Upanishad* has an equally sublime introductory scene, forming a noble background for the great teaching imparted in the *Upanishad* itself.

Vajasravasa performed an elaborate sacrifice, which terminated with a parting of all his possessions as gifts to the guests assembled. Vajasravasa's son, Nachiketas, watched the proceedings and, as he saw the gifts being given, he was filled with the thought of the vanity of it all.

"Of what use is it," he said to himself "giving these toothless old cattle and cows past the age of bearing? Should not my father, if he is minded to give what is dear to him, give *me* away?" So he went to his father and said: "Father! To whom are you going to give me?" His father did not pay heed to the question, but went on with the routine of the great sacrifice. Nachiketas repeated the question again and again till Vajasravasa, losing patience, exclaimed without meaning anything like what he said: "You? I shall give you to Yama."

Nothing could be uttered on such a solemn occasion but must be carried out. The father was aghast at his own exclamation. Nachiketas, however, decided to go to Yama. "Many have gone before me and many yet must go after me. I go not alone to Death, and what can Yama do to me? Consider what has happened before this, and consider what is going to happen in the future. Countless are the mortals that have died before this and will die hereafter. The life of mortals, indeed, is like that of the corn which grows and ripens and is reaped, and like the grains that fall which spring again into life."

बहूनामेमि प्रथमो बहूनामेमि मध्यमः ।
किंस्विद्यमस्य कर्तव्यं यन्मयाद्य करिष्यति ॥

(1)-5

अनुपश्य यथा पूर्वे प्रतिपश्य तथाऽपरे ।
सस्यमिव मर्त्यः पच्यते सस्यमिवजायतेपुनः ॥

(1)-6

So Nachiketas went to Yama. Yama was not prepared for the voluntary visitor. He was not willing to receive anyone before time. Nachiketas had to wait for three days before Yama received him. A Brahamana could not thus be disregarded even by Yama. So, to make up for the offence, Death offered to Nachiketas whatever boon he might demand. He offered many gifts—length of days, and all the possessions of the earth that one could desire, and *Swarga* thereafter. But the youth chose for a boon—instruction at Yama's hands about the nature of the soul.

"There is no boon that I desire other than this knowledge," said Nachiketas, "and there can be no better instructor than you for imparting this knowledge. What use is length of days and what joy can possessions, or song or dance, or horses and chariots give, so long as you are there as an ever-present termination to it all?"

Yama pleaded with Nachiketas:

देवैरत्रापि विचिकित्सितं पुरा
न हि सुविज्ञेयमणुरेष धर्मः ।
अन्यं वरं नचिकेतो वृणीष्व
मा मोपरोत्सीरति मा सृजैनम् ॥

Even the gods have had doubts in the matter. The nature of it is so subtle that it is not possible to comprehend it satisfactorily. Choose some other

boon, Nachiketas. Do not insist; release me from this.

(1)-21

But Nachiketas answered:

देवैरत्रापि विचिकित्सितं किल
त्वं च मृत्यो यन्न सुविज्ञेयमात्थ ।
वक्ता चास्य त्वादृगन्यो न लभ्यो
नान्यो वरस्तुल्य एतस्य कश्चित् ॥

If even the gods had doubts in this matter and you say that it is not easily to be comprehended, who then could expound it as you can, O Death, and what other boon can equal this? None, indeed.

(1)-22

Yama pleaded again:

शतायुषः पुत्रपौत्रान्वृणीष्व
बहून्पशून्हस्तिहिरण्यमश्वान् ।
भूमेर्महदायतनं वृणीष्व
स्वयं च जीव शरदो यावदिच्छसि ॥

Ask for sons and grandsons who may live for a hundred years. Ask for numerous cows, elephants, and gold and horses. Ask for large tracts of land, and live as many autumns as you desire.

(1)-23

एतत्तुल्यं यदि मन्यसे वरं
वृणीष्व वित्तं चिरजीविकां च ।
महाभूमौ नचिकेतस्त्वमेधि
कामानां त्वा कामभाजं करोमि ॥

Or choose any boon that you can conceive equal to this, with wealth and long life. Be lord of wide dominions, O Nachiketas, I will make you the enjoyer of every desire.

(1)-24

ये ये कामा दुर्लभा मर्त्यलोके
सर्वान्कामांश्छन्दतः प्रार्थयस्व ।
इमा रामाः सरथाः सतूर्या
न हीदृशा लम्भनीया मनुष्यैः ।
आभिर्मत्प्रत्ताभिः परिचारयस्व
नचिकेतो मरणं मानुप्राक्षीः ॥

Ask freely for every rare enjoyment in the world of mortals. Here are nymphs in chariots playing on lutes, such as men have never seen.

These will serve you at my command. But, do not ask me about Death.

(1)-25

Nachiketas was unmoved. He said:

श्वोभावा मर्त्यस्य यदन्तकैत-
त्सर्वेन्द्रियाणां जरयन्ति तेजः ।
अपि सर्वं जीवितमल्पमेव
तवैव वाहास्तव नृत्यगीते ॥

These ephemeral pleasures, O Death, consume the powers of the mortal's senses. Even if they lasted all life, they are of little worth. You say you give me these gifts, but being all limited by the death of the enjoyer, they remain but yours though you appear to give them away, these chariots, and song and dance.*

(1)-26

न वित्तेन तर्पणीयो मनुष्यो
लप्स्यामहे वित्तमद्राक्ष्म चेत्त्वा ।
जीविष्यामो यावदीशिष्यसि त्वं
वरस्तु मे वरणीयः स एव ॥

---

* Sri Sankaracharya's interpretation of तवैव वाहाः etc. is simply Keep these ephemeral things for yourself; I do not care for them.

How can man be satisfied with wealth? Can we hold wealth when we see you? All wealth disappears on death. We live but as long as you command it to be. That boon alone, therefore, is worthy of being desired that I craved of you.

(1)-27

Yama thus failed to persuade Nachiketas to give up his inquiry into the mystery of life even for all the pleasures of this world and of the world of the gods. "You have displayed courage and resolve," said Yama. "There can be no better seeker than such a one, even as you stated that there can be no better instructor than myself. Listen, then, I shall explain."

Then follows the teaching.

The first thing that man should learn in the pursuit of Truth is that the good is something different from the pleasant. So Yama begins thus:

अन्यच्छ्रेयोऽन्यदुतैव प्रेयस्ते
उभे नानार्थे पुरुषं सिनीतः।
तयोः श्रेय आददानस्य साधु
भवति हीयतेऽर्थाद्य उ प्रेयो वृणीते ॥

श्रेयश्च प्रेयश्च मनुष्यमेतस्तौ
संपरीत्य विविनक्ति धीरः ।
श्रेयो हि धीरोऽभिप्रेयसो वृणीते
प्रेयो मन्दो योगक्षेमाद्* वृणीते ॥

The Good is one thing, the Pleasant is another. These two lead man to very different ends. He who chooses the Good attains happiness. He who prefers the Pleasant ever loses his object. The wise are not deceived by the attractions of the Pleasant. They choose the Good. Fools are snared into the mere pleasant and perish.

(2)-1, 2

अविद्यायामन्तरे वर्तमानाः
स्वयं धीराः पण्डितंमन्यमानाः ।
दन्द्रम्यमाणाः परियन्ति मूढा
अन्धेनैव नीयमाना यथान्धाः ॥

Steeped in ignorance, men engage themselves in activities and pursuits and considering themselves men of understanding and learned, stagger

* योगक्षेमात् is explained by Sri Sankaracharya to mean "for the sake of the maintenance of the body." It may, perhaps, with a little grammatical licence, be understood to mean "hoping that the source of pleasure may be acquired and preserved."

along aimlessly like blind men led by the blind, going round and round in the cycle of births.

(2)-5

The main obstacle in the path of the man striving for the higher life is the identification of oneself with the body. Therefore, all teaching in Hindu Vedanta stresses on man finding his soul within. If one realizes the divinity of the eternal spirit within, the battle is won.

तं दुर्दर्शं गूढमनुप्रविष्टं
गुहाहितं गह्वरेष्ठं पुराणम् ।
अध्यात्मयोगाधिगमेन देवं
मत्वा धीरो हर्षशोकौ जहाति ॥

Concentrating the mind on the Spirit within, man should realize the divine character of his own soul and its inherent freedom. The Spirit lodged within oneself is unperceived because of the perplexities of joy and grief and attachment to worldly objects. When one realizes the divine Spirit within himself, all the confusion of joy and grief disappears.

(2)-12

नायमात्मा प्रवचनेन लभ्यो
न मेधया न बहुना श्रुतेन ।
यमेवैष वृणुते तेन लभ्य–
स्तस्यैष आत्मा विवृणुते तनूं स्वाम् ॥
नाविरतो दुश्चरितान् नाशान्तो नासमाहितः ।
नाशान्तमानसो वापि प्रज्ञानेनैनमाप्नुयात् ॥

This realization can come only if from inside one's own heart spring purity of resolve and earnestness of spirit. It does not come by study or learned discussions. It comes to one whose Self yearns for realization, and whose mind has turned away from evil and has learnt to subdue itself and to be at peace with the world.

(2)-23, 24

In other words, it comes out of the longing for self-realization that leads to detachment, rather than from much learning; that is to say, it comes out of the grace of the Supreme Spirit that dwells within us.

The Self is other than the changing body. It is other than the fears and the passions that agitate the mind. The Soul is divine in origin. It is not altered in nature by the qualities of the mind in which it is embodied. It can be released from the meshes of these qualities by a realization of its own intrinsic divine nature.

The reader may note that the following verses are almost identical with the Gita verses on the subject, though there is no question here of inducing Nachiketas to take up arms without any compunctions of conscience.

न जायते म्रियते वा विपश्चिन्
नायं कुतश्चिन्न बभूव कश्चित्।
अजो नित्यः शाश्वतोऽयं पुराणो
न हन्यते हन्यमाने शरीरे॥

You are not born, nor do you die. You did not come from anything else, nor were made out of something other than yourself. You are unborn, eternal, everlasting and always existed. You are not slain, though the body is slain.

(2)-18

हन्ता चेन्मन्यते हन्तुं हतश्चेन्मन्यते हतम्।
उभौ तौ न विजानीतो नायं हन्ति न हन्यते॥

If you think you slay some one, or that you will be slain by some one, you are wrong in both cases. The Soul neither slays nor is slain.

(2)-19

अणोरणीयान्महतो महीया-
नात्मास्य जन्तोर्निहितो गुहायाम् ।
तमक्रतुः पश्यति वीतशोको
धातुः प्रसादान्महिमानमात्मनः ।

Subtler than the atom, greater than the greatest, the Atman resides in the hearts of living beings. He who makes himself desireless and has cast off grief beholds the greatness of the Spirit within him.

(2)-20

अशरीरं शरीरेष्वनवस्थेष्ववस्थितम् ।
महान्तं विभुमात्मानं मत्वा धीरो न शोचति ॥

The man of understanding realizes this bodiless Spirit dwelling in the bodies, this imperishable substance lodged in the perishable and realizing it casts off grief.

(2)-21

आत्मानं रथिनं विद्धि शरीरं रथमेव तु ।
बुद्धिं तु सारथिं विद्धि मनः प्रग्रहमेव च ॥
इन्द्रियाणि हयानाहुर्विषयांस्तेषु गोचरान् ।
आत्मेन्द्रियमनोयुक्तं भोक्तेत्याहुर्मनीषिणः ॥

यस्त्वविज्ञानवान्भवत्ययुक्तेन मनसा सदा ।
तस्येन्द्रियाण्यवश्यानि दुष्टाश्वा इव सारथेः ॥
विज्ञानसारथिर्यस्तु मनः प्रग्रहवान्नरः ।
सोऽध्वनः पारमाप्नोति तद्विष्णोः परमं पदम् ॥

The journey of life can be safely completed, and the Supreme world of Vishnu reached only if one keeps a watchful control over the senses. The body is like a chariot to which the senses are yoked like horses. The mind is like the reins, which enable the charioteer, *viz.*, the understanding, to hold the horses, i.e., the senses, in check. The Soul rides on the chariot, and the road is the world of objects over which the senses move. If the reins are not held firmly and wisely, the senses, like vicious horses, will get out of control, and the chariot will not reach the goal, but will go round and round in births and re-births. If the man is wise, and controls his mind, his senses will be like good horses driven by a good driver.

(3)-3,4,5,9

पराञ्चि खानि व्यतृणत्स्वयंभू-
स्तस्मात् पराङ् पश्यति नान्तरात्मन् ।
कश्चिद्धीरः प्रत्यगात्मानमैक्षत्
आवृत्तचक्षुरमृतत्वमिच्छन् ॥

पराचः कामाननुयन्ति बालास्ते
मृत्योर्यन्ति विततस्य पाशम्।
अथ धीरा अमृतत्वं विदित्वा
ध्रुवमध्रुवेष्विह न प्रार्थयन्ते ॥

The self-existent Spirit worked its way out from within and thus the openings of the mind are directed outwards, *viz.*, the sense organs. Therefore do men's thoughts ever tend outwards. But the few, who have true understanding, turn their mind inwards and realize the Self within. Those without understanding, who do not control themselves and pursue external pleasures fall into the widespread net of Birth and Death. Those of steady mind, realizing what is truly lasting, do not turn their thoughts to transient pleasures.

(4)-1, 2

अरण्योर्निहितो जातवेदा
गर्भ इव सुभृतो गर्भिणीभिः।
दिवे दिव ईड्यो जागृवद्भिर्हविष्मद्भि-
र्मनुष्येभिरग्निरेतद्वै तत् ॥
अग्निर्यथैको भुवनं प्रविष्टो
रूपं रूपं प्रतिरूपो बभूव।
एकस्तथा सर्वभूतान्तरात्मा
रूपं रूपं प्रतिरूपो बहिश्च ॥

The sacred fire is well concealed in the wood like a child in the womb of the mother. The Soul is contained in the body as the fire is contained and concealed in the wood. Fire manifest takes shape in accordance with the thing burning. It is now the flame of a lamp, now a furnace and now a forest-fire, according as to where it is manifested. The fire by itself is one and the same. So also, the Soul though manifold in embodiment, is the same as that in which it abides for the time being.

(4)-8, (5)-9

यदेवेह तदमुत्र यदमुत्र तदन्विह ।
मृत्योः स मृत्युमाप्नोति य इह नानेव पश्यति ॥
मनसैवेदमाप्तव्यं नेह नानास्ति किंचन ।
मृत्योः स मृत्युं गच्छति य इह नानेव पश्यति ॥

What is here is there, and what is there is here; i.e., things and beings seem various but are, indeed one Being. We are liberated when we perceive this oneness. We go from death to death if we perceive difference. It is the mind that by enlightenment can overcome the notion of difference and have a vision of the transcendent Oneness of all.

(4)-10, 11

यथोदकं दुर्गे वृष्टं पर्वतेषु विधावति ।
एवं धर्मान्पृथक् पश्यंस्तानेवानुविधावति ॥
यथोदकं शुद्धे शुद्धमासिक्तं तादृगेव भवति ।
एवं मुनेर्विजानत आत्मा भवति गौतम ॥

The rain falling on the hill divides itself and flows down the hill-sides in many torrents. The ignorant man sees manifoldness in beings and is confused and he runs after the manifoldness. If water is poured into water, it becomes one and the same with it. Thus it is with the Self of the man of understanding who sees unity in manifoldness.

(4)-14, 15

It is the light of the Spirit within that really enables us to see, not the light that falls from outside. Does this Spirit within shine by its own light or does it shine by Another Light? Is it a Self-luminous Soul or is it a reflection of the One lustrous Being? It is on this note of sublime doubt that the fifth *valli* of the *Upanishad* closes. The following two verses go together:

तदेतदिति मन्यन्तेऽनिर्देश्यं परमं सुखम् ।
कथं नु तद्विजानीयां किमु भाति विभाति वा ।

They say that the Indefinable Spirit of Supreme Bliss is this that is within me. How can I make out whether this Spirit within me shines by itself or shines by the reflected light from the Universal Spirit?

(5)-14

न तत्र सूर्यो भाति न चन्द्रतारकं
नेमा विद्युतो भान्ति कुतोऽयमग्निः ।
तमेव भान्तमनुभाति सर्वं
तस्य भासा सर्वमिदं विभाति ॥

The sun does not furnish the light there, nor the moon, nor the stars, nor these flashes of lightning born of the clouds; certainly not the light of these sacrificial fires. The Spirit shines and all things else shine as a result. Everything in the universe reflects but that light.*

(5)-15

Merely to know is not enough to escape from the tangle of illusion. Faith and discipline of life

* I crave the forgiveness of the learned for giving an interpretation different from the orthodox commentarians in regard to these two verses. My interpretation is based on the juxtaposition of भाति and विभाति.

are necessary. The illusion arises not so much from ignorance as from attachments. Enlightenment comes with detachment, not with learning. This is the main teaching to which all the schools of Hindu philosophy ultimately revert and on which they lay the greatest emphasis. The discipline and meditation that serve to help the Soul to detach itself from the things or the world is what is called *Yoga*.

यदा सर्वे प्रभिद्यन्ते हृदयस्येह ग्रन्थयः ।
अथ मर्त्योऽमृतो भवत्येतावद्ध्यनुशासनम् ॥

When the knots of the heart are untied, and man is freed from wordly attachments, he becomes immortal. This is the whole of the teaching.

(6)-15

The *Antaratman* is lodged in the secret recess of our hearts. It is sheathed as the reed-plant is sheathed in its blades. We should abstract it with understanding, tearing ourselves from attachments and desires and separating the pure from the gross. The Spirit within is pure and is immortal. Thus ends Yama's exhortation in this *Upanishad*:

अंगुष्ठमात्रः पुरुषोऽन्तरात्मा
सदा जनानां हृदये संनिविष्टः ।
तं स्वाच्छरीरात्प्रवृहेन्मुञ्जादिवेषीकां धैर्येण ।
तं विद्याच्छुक्रममृतं तं विद्याच्छुक्रममृतमिति ॥

Of the size of a thumb, the Spirit within is lodged in the hearts of men and is there always. With understanding, separate Him from the sheaths of the body in which He is lodged, even as you take off the blades of a reed-plant. Know that He is immaculate and deathless.

(6)-17

ISAVASYOPANISHAD

THE *Bhagavad Gita* presents a synthesis of the highest spiritual effort of the individual with the most practical social co-operation. We should carry on the activities of life, but we should do so remembering that all that we do belongs to God. Work done in this spirit will not cling to us in rebirth. This teaching that is expanded in the *Bhagavad Gita* is found tersely enunciated in the *Isavasyopanishad* in the first two verses.

ॐ ईशावास्यमिदं सर्वं यत्किं च जगत्यां जगत् ।
तेन त्यक्तेन भुञ्जीथा मा गृधः कस्य स्विद्धनम् ॥
कुर्वन्नेवेह कर्माणि जिजीविषेच्छतं समाः ।
एवं त्वयि नान्यथेतोऽस्ति न कर्म लिप्यते नरे ॥

Everything in the universe abides in the Supreme Being. Realize this well, and, realizing it, cast off the desires that rise in the heart, for example, the thought of possessing what is enjoyed by another. Joy comes only by the giving up of desires and attachments. You may live the longest life, doing work in a detached spirit and dedicating everything to God. Thus only can we

escape the contamination of work and sterilize life.

1, 2

The Vedantic teaching about higher knowledge should not confuse us into neglect of duties and indifference about discipline of mind and control of senses. To go through the activities of daily life in a spirit of detachment serves as a preparation for the reception of higher knowledge and for self-realization which secures *Moksha*. Indeed, philosophical learning without discipline of conduct is more to be dreaded than even ritualism without the knowledge of *Vedanta*. Higher enlightenment is impossible, and even if it were possible, worthless, unless there has been preparation and purification by means of restraint of the senses. Fill the span of life given to you, says the *Upanishad*, with work and worship as is done by people without the higher knowledge, but carry on the work in the spirit of detachment and understand the forms in the sense that you have learnt from the higher knowledge. Thereby you shall pass through Death to Immortality.

अन्धं तमः प्रविशन्ति येऽविद्यामुपासते ।
ततो भूय इव ते तमो य उ विद्यायां रताः ॥

9

विद्यां चाविद्यां च यस्तद्वेदोभयं सह।
अविद्यया मृत्युं तीर्त्वा विद्ययाऽमृतमश्नुते* ॥

11

The *Santi Sloka* of this *Upanishad* tersely sets out the relation of the Individual Soul to the Supreme Spirit. The Self that functions within us is of divine origin. It is of the same substance as the Supreme Spirit. The part that makes up the individual comes out of the whole, and the stuff of which it is made is of such a transcendental nature that the whole remains whole, in spite of something being taken out of the whole. Again, though what is taken out is but a part, it is as whole as the original. The axioms of mathematics relating to the whole and the part do not apply to the Absolute and its manifestations.

ॐ पूर्णमदः पूर्णमिदं पूर्णात्पूर्णमुदच्यते।
पूर्णस्य पूर्णमादाय पूर्णमेवावशिष्यते ॥

---

* *Vidya* and *Avidya* are phrases presenting considerable difficulty and the context does not help to clarify doubts. But I venture to think that the purport of the two *slokas* is what I have given above.

That is whole and this is whole. The perfect has come out of the perfect. Yet the perfect remains, as before, perfect.

As the Soul is the life of the body which without it would be a carcase, so is the Supreme Spirit the essence of the individual Soul's being. And yet, even as the Soul is 'lost' in the body, the Supreme Spirit, functioning as the Soul of the Individual Soul, loses cognizance of its own real Divine nature. It is the Supreme Spirit that moves, though in reality there is no motion, it being the one Reality. There can be no motion when there is nought else. It is far away, because we fail to realize it. It is near, because it is immanent in everything and is in the recess of one's own heart.

तदेजति तन्नैजति तद्दूरे तद्वन्तिके ।
तदन्तरस्य सर्वस्य तदु सर्वस्यास्य बाह्यतः ॥

It moves. It does not move. It is far away, yet most near. It is the internal Spirit of everything that we know.

If we realize this all-pervading immanence of the Supreme Spirit, the distinction between oneself and others melts away and with it disappear, as a matter of course, grief and illusion. The 29th and following verses in the sixth chapter of the

Bhagavad Gita are almost in the same words as the following *slokas* from *Isavasyopanishad*:

यस्तु सर्वाणि भूतान्यात्मन्येवानुपश्यति ।
सर्वभूतेषु चात्मानं ततो न विजुगुप्सते ॥

If one sees all living things as if they were in his own body, i.e., feels their joys and sorrows as his own, and sees the same Universal Spirit in all things then there is no need for protecting oneself against others.

6

यस्मिन्सर्वाणि भूतान्यात्मैवाभूद्विजानतः ।
तत्र को मोहः कः शोक एकत्वमनुपश्यतः ॥

When a man understands that all beings are, indeed, the all-pervading Spirit, then he realizes the oneness of all things and illusion and grief vanish.

7

The *Isavasyopanishad* emphasises the need for balance. In verses which are unfortunately obscure (9, 11, 12, and 14), the importance of both knowledge and discipline, and of attention to matter as well as to spirit is dealt with.

The *Upanishad* winds up with a prayer for strength to maintain internal and external purity.

Addressing the morning sun, the aspirant is taught to feel and say, "O Sun, of refulgent glory, I am the same Person as He that is in you." And he is asked to say to himself: "My body will disintegrate but not I and my deeds. O Mind, remember this always, remember this always."

पूषन्नेकर्षे यम सूर्य प्राजापत्य
व्यूह रश्मीन्समूह तेजः ।
यत्ते रूपं कल्याणतमं तत्ते पश्यामि
योऽसावसौ पुरुषः सोऽहमस्मि ॥

Oh Sun, who art our Nourisher, Giver of Knowledge, Dispenser of Justice, Giver of Light, Son of the Creator, disperse thy rays, draw in thy light, so that I may be enabled to behold thy most beautiful form. I am that same Person as makes thee who thou art.

16

As for my body:

वायुरनिलममृतमथेदं भस्मान्तं शरीरम् ।
ॐ क्रतो स्मर कृतं स्मर क्रतो स्मर कृतं स्मर ॥

My body will be reduced to ashes and my breath will join the deathless moving winds. Oh Mind, remember thy acts.

17

The formula—I am the person that is seen in that refulgent form—occurs slightly modified in *Chhandogya Upanishad* also. The insistence is on the realization of the all-inclusive Oneness of the Soul, the Universe. The Spirit in the Sun is the same as myself! A daily repetition and contemplation of this truth is prescribed as an aid in life to detachment, elevation of Spirit and Self-realization.

KENOPANISHAD

WHAT is the Supreme Spirit? By what relation to our experience shall we understand it? This is the subject of enquiry in this *Upanishad*. As the *Isavasyopanishad* is known by its first word, so also is this *Upanishad* named after its first word *Kena*, "By whom?"

Neither by the senses nor by human reasoning can we hope to comprehend the nature of *Brahman*. This is so because the subject, the object and the means are all identical. It is *Brahman* by which the understanding itself functions.

यन्मनसा न मनुते येनाहुर्मनो मतम् ।
तदेव ब्रह्म त्वं विद्धि नेदं यदिदमुपासते ॥
यच्चक्षुषा न पश्यति येन चक्षूंषि पश्यति ।
तदेव ब्रह्म त्वं विद्धि नेदं यदिदमुपासते ॥
यच्छ्रोत्रेण न शृणोति येन श्रोत्रमिदं श्रुतम् ।
तदेव ब्रह्म त्वं विद्धि नेदं यदिदमुपासते ॥
यत्प्राणेन न प्राणिति येन प्राणः प्रणीयते ।
तदेव ब्रह्म त्वं विद्धि नेदं यदिदमुपासते ॥

The Supreme Spirit is that by which the mind thinks; it is not one of the concepts that can be conceived by the mind, but it is that by which, indeed, one is able to think through his mind. It is that which enables the eye to see, the ear to hear, the breath to move. These functions themselves depend on *Bràhman,* and, therefore, are these senses and the mind unable to comprehend the *Brahman.* Do not take this body that one has to feed and look after for the Soul.

Life is not the aggregate of the functions of the body but a function of the Highest Spirit, inasmuch as not a thought or a breath or a glance is possible without the Supreme Agent.

1-5, 6, 7, 8

यदि मन्यसे सुवेदेति दभ्रमे–
वापि नूनं त्वं वेत्थ ब्रह्मणो रूपम्।
यदस्य त्वं यदस्य च देवेष्वथ नु
मीमांस्यमेव ते मन्ये विदितम्॥
यस्यामतं तस्य मतं मतं यस्य न वेद सः।
अविज्ञातं विजानतां विज्ञातमविजानताम्॥

NOTE : I have interpreted नेदं यदिदमुपासते as above on the lines of Sri Ramanujacharya's commentary on the first six chapters of the Gita.

He who thinks that he knows really thereby proves himself ignorant. He who realizes that he cannot know Him has best understood him. Those who seek to know Him, as they can grasp things of ordinary knowledge, can never achieve their object. Those who realize the limitation of the human mind in respect of the knowledge of the Supreme Spirit and, therefore, frankly confess ignorance, really approach a true understanding of it.

II-1, 3

The limitation of human knowledge, when trying to comprehend the Supreme Being, is brought out in the above epigram.

प्रतिबोधविदितं मतममृतत्वं हि विन्दते।
आत्मना विन्दते वीर्यं विद्यया विन्दतेऽमृतम् ॥

Not by reasoning but only by an awakening can we get a vision of the Supreme Spirit. Life, in relation to the Ultimate Reality, is like a state of sleep. Reason, in respect of Ultimate Reality, is like the impossible conception of a sleeping man trying to know what he is about, without waking up. As sleep is to waking, so is ordinary life to the state of realization.

Self-discipline gives strength of spirit: आत्मना विन्दते वीर्यं. To one so strengthened, knowledge gives immortality: विद्यया विन्दतेऽमृतम् ।

The Self is itself immortal, and one has but to know it to become immortal. A man dreams that he is suffering from a mortal illness and is dying. He suffers pain and even death. But the moment he wakes up, he is cured and regains life. So does *Jnana* give immortality to man.

The third chapter of this *Upanishad* is an allegory to illustrate that everything rests on the Supreme Spirit. It is That which gives heat to Fire, and energy to Motion, and the power of knowing to individual knowledge, however great. All beings are like electric lamps that glow by the power that is received by them from the Supreme Being, themselves not knowing it.

The gods were once elated at a great victory, and the *Brahman* appeared before them. They could not recognize or understand the vision. Agni, Vayu and Indra were sent to approach and understand Him. They went, one by one, and tried to impress on the strange vision their respective powers. But when they were challenged to prove their vaunted strength, *Agni* could not burn, and *Vayu* could not move by a hair's breadth a dry bit of grass which was placed before them and which they attacked with all their strength one after the other. *Indra* went near to see, when the other two failed, but with his thousand eyes he failed to see anything whatsoever. The apparition disappeared altogether from his sight.

तेऽग्निमब्रुवञ्जातवेद एतद्विजानीहि
किमेतद्यक्षमिति तथेति ॥

The said to *Agni*: "Oh, Jataveda, go and ascertain who this is, this adorable Being." He said: "Yes."

III-3

तदभ्यद्रवत्तमभ्यवदत्कोऽसीत्यग्निर्वा
अहमस्मीत्यब्रवीज्जातवेदा वा अहमस्मीति ॥

He ran up to the Being, who asked him: "Who are you?" *Agni* answered: "I am *Agni*, I am also called Jataveda."

III-4

तस्मिंस्त्वयि किं वीर्यमित्यपीदं
सर्वं दहेयं यदिदं पृथिव्यामिति ।

"And what is your strength?", the Being asked. "I can burn up all that is here on earth," answered Agni.

III-5

तस्मै तृणं निदधावेतद्दहेति
तदुपप्रेयाय सर्वजवेन तन्न शशाक दग्धुं ।
स तत एव निववृते
नैतदशकं विज्ञातुं यदेतद्यक्षमिति ॥

He placed before *Agni* a bit of dry grass, saying, "Burn this." Going at it with all his energy *Agni* found that he could not burn it. He returned to the gods and said he could not make out who this strange Being was.

III-6

अथ वायुमब्रुवन्वायवेतद्विजानीहि
किमेतद्यक्षमिति तथेति ॥

Then they said to *Vayu*: "Oh, do go ascertain who this is." And *Vayu* said: "So be it."

III-7

तदभ्यद्रवत्तमभ्यवदत्कोऽसीति वायुर्वा
अहमस्मीत्यब्रवीन्मातरिश्वा वा अहमस्मीति ॥

He ran up to the Being, who asked him: "Who are you?" "I am *Vayu*, otherwise called Matarisva," answered *Vayu*.

III-8

तस्मिंस्त्वयि किं वीर्यमित्यपीदं
सर्वमाददीयं यदिदं पृथिव्यामिति ॥

Then said the Being: "What is your strength?" "Oh, I can sweep away whatever exists on this earth," answered *Vayu.*

III-9

तस्मै तृणं निदधावेतदादत्स्वेति
तदुपप्रेयाय सर्वजवेन तन्न
शशाकादातुं स तत एव निववृते
नैतदशकं विज्ञातुं यदेतद्यक्षमिति ॥

Then the Being placed a withered blade of grass before *Vayu,* and said: "Move this." *Vayu* set on it with all his might, but could not move it; and he returned to the gods and said: "I could not make out who this is."

III-10

अथेन्द्रमब्रुवन्मघवन्नेत–
द्विजानीहि किमेतद्यक्षमिति
तथेति तदभ्यद्रवत्तस्मात्तिरोदधे ॥

Thereupon, they beseeched *Indra* to find out who it was. He agreed to do so, but when he ran up, he found that the Being had gone out of his view altogether.

III-11

SVETASVATAROPANISHAD

THE dotrine of the Vedanta is summarized in the following *mantras*:

संयुक्तमेतत्क्षरमक्षरं च
व्यक्ताव्यक्तं भरते विश्वमीशः ।
अनीशश्चात्मा बध्यते भोक्तृभावा-
ज्ज्ञात्वा देवं मुच्यते सर्वपाशैः ॥

The Lord upholds the Universe, which is a union of the manifest and the unmanifest, the imperishable and the perishable. Functioning as Enjoyer through the senses, the Soul in man loses the consciousness of lordship and is enchained. When he realizes lordship, he is freed from every tie. Let man realize the Divinity of his soul. Thereby does he obtain Release.

1-8

क्षरं प्रधानममृताक्षरं हरः
क्षरात्मानावीशते देव एकः ।
तस्याभिध्यानाद्योजनात्तत्वभावाद्
भूयश्चान्ते विश्वमायानिवृत्तिः ॥

Iswara rules over the Soul as well as material nature which forms the field for the Soul's functioning. Man reaches liberation from all the illusions of the world by contemplation and repeated meditation until realization is attained of the true nature of these three, God, Matter and Soul.

I-10

The fire is not seen when it is concealed in the wood. But it appears to view when the wood burns. So does meditation bring out the Supreme Spirit from within us. Like oil hidden in the sesame seed, like *ghee* concealed in milk, like water hidden from view in the river-bed, like fire that is contained in the *Arani* (fire-churner), abides the Supreme Spirit within us, though not manifest. When the two pieces of wood in the *Arani* are rubbed, the fire manifests itself. The butter is separated by churning the milk. The water is seen if we sink a pit in the sand of the river-bed. The Divine Self, that is hidden within one's self, can similarly be made manifest through the practice of truth, meditation and control of mind and senses, which is penance. Make the body the lower piece of the *Arani* and make the Understanding the upper piece, and by the practice of meditation, churn the fire out, so to say.

वह्नेर्यथा योनिगतस्य मूर्तिर्न
दृश्यते नैव च लिङ्गनाशः।
स भूय एवेन्धनयोनिगृह्य–
स्तद्वोभयं वै प्रणवेन देहे॥

Just as fire when it abides in its womb, the woods, is not seen in its manifest form but yet exists and appears to view when the wood burns, even so do both aspects of abiding unmanifest and being drawn out apply to the Spirit in the body. The *Pranava* can enable the Spirit to be perceived.

I-13

स्वदेहमरणिं कृत्वा प्रणवं चोत्तरारणिम्।
ध्याननिर्मथनाभ्यासात् देवं पश्येन्निगूढवत्॥

Make your body the nether piece and *Pranava* the uppeer piece of the *Arani* and churn with the practice of meditation. Thus will you be enabled to perceive the concealed Divinity within.

I-14

तिलेषु तैलं दधनीव सर्पिरापः
स्रोतस्स्वरणीषु चाग्निः।

एवमात्मात्मनि गृह्यतेऽसौ
सत्येनैनं तपसा योऽनुपश्यति ॥

As oil in the oil-seed, *ghee* in the curdled milk and water in the river-bed, so can That be obtained out of the self, through truth and restraint of thought and the senses.

1-15

The following verses are addressed as a prayer for enlightenment to the Universal Spirit which is One but takes various shapes with various powers and functions, that will in the end re-unite and be lost in Him—the Sun, the Moon, the Air, the starry firmament, fire, water, Brahma, the Lord, man and woman, in youth or in tottering old age, beast, bird, insect, the dark-blue bee, the green parrot with red eyes, the clouds that shoot forth lightning, the ocean, the seasons—all will be re-absorbed in Him that has no beginning, the cause of All.

य एकोऽवर्णो बहुधा शक्तियोगा–
द्वर्णाननेकान्निहितार्थो दधाति ।
विचैति चान्ते विश्वमादौ स देवः
स नो बुद्ध्या शुभया संयुनक्तु ॥
तदेवाग्निस्तदादित्यस्तद्वायुस्तदु चन्द्रमाः ।
तदेव शुक्रं तद्ब्रह्म तदापस्तत्प्रजापतिः ॥

त्वं स्त्री त्वं पुमानसि
त्वं कुमार उत वा कुमारी ।
त्वं जीर्णो दण्डेन वंचसि
त्वं जातो भवसि विश्वतोमुखः ॥

नीलः पतंगो हरितो लोहिताक्ष–
स्तडिद्गर्भ ऋतवः समुद्राः ।
अनादिमत्त्वं विभुत्वेन वर्तसे
यतो जातानि भुवनानि विश्वा ॥

IV 1-4

एष देवो विश्वकर्मा महात्मा
सदा जनानां हृदये संनिविष्टः ।
हृदा मनीषा मनसाऽभिक्लृप्तो
य एतद्विदुरमृतास्ते भवन्ति ॥

The Divine Spirit that has forged and brought the Universe into being, the Supreme Soul, ever dwells in the hearts of men. He is revealed by the heart and intellect combining and controlling the mind and by meditation. They attain deathlessness who thus see Him revealed.

IV-17

न संदृशे तिष्ठन्ति रूपमस्य
न चक्षुषा पश्यति कश्चनैनम् ।
हृदा हृदिस्थं मनसा य
एनमेवं विदुरमृतास्ते भवन्ति ॥

This *Isa,* dwelling in the heart of man, can be perceived not by the eye but the heart; and he who perceives Him thus by the heart attains immortality.

IV-20

Not time or innate quality of matter is the true cause of phenomena, as some learned men imagine, but the glory of God who dwells in and revolves all things, animate and inanimate. When one discovers this Universal Spirit within one's self, the misery of life is ended. It would be easier to roll up the sky and carry it on one's head as a tanner carries a hide than to achieve happiness without realizing the immanence of God.

स्वभावमेके कवयो वदन्ति
कालं तथान्ये परिमुह्यमानाः ।
देवस्यैष महिमा तु लोके
येनेदं भ्राम्यते ब्रह्मचक्रम् ॥

Some learned men attribute the phenomena of the universe to the innate nature of things, other deluded persons say that time is the cause. But it is the glory of God by which alone the wheel revolves and this world goes on.

VI-1

यदा चर्मवदाकाशं वेष्टयिष्यन्ति मानवाः ।
तदा देवमविज्ञाय दुःखस्यान्तो भविष्यति ॥

When (men could roll up the sky like a hide), we could reach the end of pain and grief without realizing God who abides in all things.

VI-20

एको देवः सर्वभूतेषु गूढः
सर्वव्यापि सर्वभूतान्तरात्मा ।
कर्माध्यक्षः सर्वभूताधिवासः
साक्षी चेता केवलो निर्गुणश्च ॥

God, who is concealed in all beings, is one. He pervades everything. He is the inner soul of every being and the overseer of all activity. He dwells in all forms of life. He is the eternal witness, the Conscious Being within, standing apart from that in which He abides and unqualified.

VI-11

निष्कलं निष्क्रियं शान्तं निरवद्यं निरंजनम् ।
अमृतस्य परं सेतुं दग्धेन्धनमिवानलम् ॥

Without parts, action-less, tranquil, uncontaminable, spotless, the bridge that transcends and leads to immortality, consuming and unquenchable like fire.

VI-19

The direct teaching of a father or a *Guru* is essential. Without this, book-knowledge would be of no great avail. But more important than all is the previous purging of character and restraint of mind and senses, which are necessary for the knowledge and realization of the highest truth. Otherwise, knowledge leads to harm, not to good. "I am God" would lead to arrogance and atheism without purity of character, restraint and humility and the personal guidance of father or revered teacher. Hence the following prohibition which should not be understood in any sense other than the caution above indicated:

वेदान्ते परमं गुह्यं पुराकल्पे प्रचोदितम् ।
नाप्रशान्ताय दातव्यम् नापुत्रायाशिष्याय वा पुनः ॥

VI-22

TAITTIRIYOPANISHAD

We have in the *Taittiriya Upanishad*, (first *valli*, eleventh *anuvaka*) a valedictory exhortation which reveals to us something of the system of education that produced the cultured among the ancient inhabitants of this sacred land.

वेदमनूच्याचार्योऽन्तेवासिनमनुशास्ति । सत्यं वद । धर्मं चर । स्वाध्यायान्मा प्रमदः । आचार्याय प्रियं धनमाहृत्य प्रजातन्तुं मा व्यवच्छेत्सीः । सत्यान्न प्रमदितव्यम् । धर्मान्न प्रमदितव्यम् । कुशलान्न प्रमदितव्यम् । भूत्यै न प्रमदितव्यम् । स्वाध्यायप्रवचनाभ्यां न प्रमदितव्यम् ॥ १ ॥

> After having taught the *Vedas*, the teacher instructs the pupil thus: Speak what is true. Do your duties. Continue, without neglect, the daily study of the *Veda*. Now that you have come to the end of your stay with your teacher, marry and bring forth progeny. Do not swerve from Truth and *Dharma*, and do something useful in the social economy. Achieve greatness, and do not fail to refresh your memory in respect of what you have learnt.

देवपितृकार्याभ्यां न प्रमदितव्यम्। मातृदेवो भव। पितृदेवो भव। आचार्यदेवो भव। अतिथिदेवो भव। यान्यनवद्यानि कर्माणि, तानि सेवितव्यानि, नो इतराणि। यान्यस्माकं सुचरितानि, तानि त्वयोपास्यानि नो इतराणि॥ ये के चास्मच्छ्रेयांसो ब्राह्मणाः तेषां त्वयाऽऽसने न प्रश्वसितव्यम्॥

Remember the gods and your ancestors. Honour your mother. Look upon her as God. Honour your father. Look upon him as God. Honour your teacher as God. Honour your guest. Look upon him as if God came to receive your attention. May you ever exercise your understanding and, distinguishing the good from the blame-worthy, avoid the latter and ever do what is good. Follow all that was good in your teacher's life, not any other. You will meet with better men than even the teachers with whom you have lived. Show them due respect.

श्रद्धया देयम्। अश्रद्धयाऽदेयम्। श्रिया देयम्। ह्रिया देयम्। भिया देयम्। संविदा देयम्।

Give gifts with faith, not neglectfully but with joy, with humility, with fear and with kindness.

अथ यदि ते कर्मविचिकित्सा वा वृत्तिविचिकित्सा वा स्यात्। ये तत्र ब्राह्मणाः संमर्शिनः, युक्ता आयुक्ताः, अलूक्षा धर्मकामाः स्युः, यथा

ते तत्र वर्तेरन् तथा तत्र वर्तेथाः। अथाभ्याख्यातेषु। तत्र ब्राह्मणा संमर्शिनः, युक्ता आयुक्ताः, अलूक्षा धर्मकामाः स्युः, यथा ते तेषु वर्तेरन् तथा तेषु वर्तेथाः। एष आदेशः। एष उपदेशः॥

If your mind is troubled with any doubt as to what is right or wrong, follow the example of gentle and pious elders living in your neighbourhood in regard to those matters. This is the rule and this the teaching.

I-11

In the third *valli* of the *Taittiriya* Upanishad, *Varuna* instructs his son *Bhrigu* on the immanence of *Brahman* in matter as well as in the Spirit. The food we eat and the air we breathe are sacred forms of *Brahman* that builds us up, enables us to speak, think, act, exercise the will and understand.

अन्नं ब्रह्मेति व्यजानात्
अन्नादेव खल्विमानि भूतानि जायन्ते।
अन्नेन जातानि जीवन्ति
अन्नं प्रयन्त्यभिसंविशन्तीति॥

He knew that food is *Brahman*, for from food, indeed, are born all beings in this world, by food do they live, and, after death, they become food again for other beings.

III-2

We should not speak ill of food. We should not throw away food. We should produce plenty of food. We should let no one who comes for food be turned away

अन्नं न निन्द्यात् । तद्व्रतम् ।
अन्नं न परिचक्षीत । तद्व्रतम् ।
अन्नं बहु कुर्वीत । तद्व्रतम् ।
न कंचन वसतौ प्रत्याचक्षीत । तद्व्रतम् ॥

III-7-10

The teaching is that food should be looked upon as *Brahman,* for from food are born all beings, by food do they live, and they become food at their death. It is by food, one for another, that all beings are made interdependent and made into one linked whole in the world.

CHHANDOGYOPANISHAD

THE sixth chapter of the *Chhandogya Upanishad* begins with the old, old riddle: Was there a first cause? Shall we, seeing that the search for causes leads us backwards along an interminable chain, give up the theory of causation and say that the world came out of nothing? This cannot be, says the *Rishi*. Out of nothing, nothing could come. Non-Being cannot produce Being. Much less could the phenomenon of consciousness come out of nothing. We must hold that there was a first Cause: *Sat: i.e.*, Being with consciousness.

Sat willed that it may expand and multiply. So it produced light, *Tejas*. The Spirit in *Tejas* willed to multiply and produced water. The Spirit in Water willed to become manifold, and it produced all the living things of the world.

Lest the reader imagine that the march of modern science has made this explanation out of date, it may be recalled that neither Chemistry nor Biology nor any other physical science *explains* anything. Plato depicted mankind as chained in a cave in such a way that they can look only on the wall which forms the back of the cave; they cannot see the busy life outside but only the shadows which objects moving in the sunshine cast on the walls of the cave. For the captives in the cave, the shadows constitute the whole phenominal world, the world of reality remaining for ever beyond their ken. Sir James Jeans, the great physicist, says that modern science has come to the same conclusion. The reality behind the phenomenal world is unreachable. Chemical and other "laws" are only classifications and simplifications of observed phenomena, and nothing more. Neither familiarity nor classification can itself be explanation. The unexplained factor outside the cave that permanently circumscribes our knowledge is the *Sat* of the Chhandogya.

"How can this vast universe with its multitudinous variety be produced in this simple way?" asked Svetaketu, whom his father, Uddalaka, was instructing as to how the entire world has been evolved out of the *Sat*.

न्यग्रोधफलमत आहरेतीदं भगव इति, भिन्धीति, भिन्नं भगव इति,
किमत्र पश्यसीत्यण्व्य इवेमा धाना भगव इत्यासामंगैकां भिन्धीति, भिन्ना
भगव इति, किमत्र पश्यसीति, न किंचन भगव इति ॥ १ ॥ तं होवाच यं वै
सोम्यैतमणिमानं न निभालयस एतस्य वै सोम्यैषोऽणिम्न एवं महान्य-
ग्रोधस्तिष्ठति, श्रद्धत्स्व सोम्येति ॥ २ ॥ स य एषोऽणिमैतदात्म्यमिदं सर्वं
तत्सत्यं स आत्मा तत्त्वमसि श्वेतकेतो इति, भूय एव मा भगवान् विज्ञापय-
त्विति, तथा सोम्येति होवाच ॥ ३ ॥

"Fetch a fruit of the big fig tree," said Uddalaka
"Here is one, Sir," said Svetaketu.
"Break it, what do you see there?"
"These little seeds."
"Crush one of the little seeds."
"Yes, Sir, I have done it."
"What do you see inside?"
"Nothing," said the son.

"Yet in the subtle substance inside that little seed, which your eye does not even perceive, existed all this big branching *nyagrodha* tree. Do you wonder at it? Likewise all that exists, this universe, was in that *Sat* which thou too art. Believe it, dear child, thou art that."

VI-(14)-1-3

"If the *Sat* is the all-pervading cause of all, why is it not perceived clearly?" is the next question.

As a lump of salt is dissolved in water and disappears, so is the *Sat* lost from view in the world but is still immanent in everything in the universe, as the salt is present in every part of the water. The following is a vivid account of the instruction in this regard, which reminds one of a modern laboratory lecture:

लवणमेतदुदकेऽवधायाथ मा प्रातरुपसीदथा इति, स ह तथा चकार;
तं होवाच यद्दोषा लवणमुदकेऽवाधा अंग तदाहरेति, तद्धावमृश्य न विवेद ॥ १ ॥
यथा विलीनमेवांगास्यान्तादाचामेति, कथमिति, लवणमिति; मध्यादाचा-
मेति, कथमिति, लवणमित्यन्तादाचामेति, कथमिति, लवणमित्यभिप्रास्यै-
तदथ मोपसीदथा इति; तद्ध तथा चकार, तच्छश्वत्संवर्तते, तं होवाचात्र
वाव किल सत्सोम्य न निभालयसेऽत्रैव किलेति ॥ २ ॥ स य एषोऽणिमैतदा-
त्म्यमिदं सर्वं तत्सत्यं स आत्मा तत्त्वमसि श्वेतकेतो इति, भूय एव मा भगवान्
विज्ञापयत्विति, तथा सोम्येति होवाच ॥ ३ ॥

VI-(12)-1-3

"How are we to gain knowledge of the *Sat*, which is imperceptible?" is the next question.

यथा सोम्य पुरुषं गन्धारेभ्योऽभिनद्धाक्षमानीय तं ततोऽतिजने
विसृजेत्स यथा तत्र प्राङ्वोदङ्वाऽधराङ्वा प्रत्यङ्वा प्रध्मायीताभिनद्धाक्षो
आनीतोऽभिनद्धाक्षो विसृष्टः ॥ १ ॥ तस्य यथाभिनहनं प्रमुच्य प्रब्रूयादेतां
दिशं गन्धारा एतां दिशं व्रजेति, स ग्रामाद्ग्रामं पृच्छन् पण्डितो मेधावी गन्धारा-
नेवोपसंपद्येतैवमेवेहाचार्यवान् पुरुषो वेद, तस्य तावदेव चिरं यावन्न विमोक्ष्येऽथ
संपत्स्य इति ॥ २ ॥ स य एषोऽणिमैतदात्म्यमिदं सर्वं तत्सत्यं स आत्मा
तत्त्वमसि श्वेतकेतो इति, भूय एव मा भगवान्विज्ञापयत्विति, तथा सोम्येति
होवाच ॥ ३ ॥

Like unto that of a man blindfolded and carried away by robbers from his own country is man's condition. The folds of cloth over his eyes being removed by a friend, he recovers the use of his eyes and slowly finds his way home, step by step, enquiring at each stage. So also, the good teacher instructs the seeker of Truth and helps him to unloose his bonds of desire, and saves him from the robbers. The robbers are his past deeds that brought him to this condition. Recovering his sight as soon as the desires and attachments that blind his vision are removed, he finds his way to the *Sat*. Thereafter, it is only a matter of waiting for natural death.

VI-(14)-1-3

MUNDAKOPANISHAD

ॐ भद्रं कर्णेभिः शृणुयाम देवा भद्रं पश्येमाक्षभिर्यजत्राः ।। स्थिरै-
रंगैस्तुष्टुवांसस्तनूभिर्व्यशेमहि देवहितं यदायुः । स्वस्ति न इन्द्रो वृद्धश्रवाः
स्वस्ति नः पूषा विश्ववेदाः । स्वस्ति नस्तार्क्ष्यो अरिष्टनेमिः स्वस्ति नो
बृहस्पतिर्दधातु ।। ॐ शान्तिः शान्तिः शान्तिः ।।

May our ears hear what is good, may our eyes see what is good. May we, what time we live, be blessed with healthy limbs and body, that we may glorify the lord. May all the gods bless us. May our minds be at peace.

This *Upanishad* consists of Angiras's instruction to his disciple, Shaunaka.

तस्मै स होवाच । द्वे विद्ये वेदितव्ये इतिहस्म यद्ब्रह्मविदो वदन्ति,
परा चैवापरा च ।। ४ ।। तत्रापरा ऋग्वेदो यजुर्वेदः सामवेदोऽथर्ववेदः शिक्षा
कल्पो व्याकरणं निरुक्तं छन्दो ज्योतिषमिति । अथ परा, यया तदक्षरमधि-
गम्यते ।। ५ ।।

There are two sciences worthy of being learnt, of which the learned treat one as higher, and the other as lower. The *Vedas*, the *Rig Veda*, the *Yajur Veda*, the *Sama Veda*, the *Atharva Veda*, intonation, ritual, grammar, etymology, metre, astronomy and all else that is commonly known as learning constitute the lower knowledge, the higher is that by which the Ever-existing is realised.*

I-(1)-4, 5

प्लावा ह्येते अदृढा यज्ञरूपा अष्टादशोक्तमवरं येषु कर्म। एतच्छ्रेयो येऽभिनन्दन्ति मूढा जरामृत्युं ते पुनरेवापि यन्ति ॥ ७ ॥ अविद्यायामन्तरे वर्तमानाः स्वयं धीराः पण्डितंमन्यमानाः। जंघन्यमानाः परियन्ति मूढा अन्धेनैव नीयमाना यथान्धाः ॥ ८ ॥

Ceremonials and sacrifices lead men round and round, and not to the ultimate goal to which an understanding of the Self alone can lead.

The popular belief as regards the efficacy of sacrifices is, though not rudely negatived, politely put aside in the *Upanishads* as not leading to what is true and imperishable happiness.

The passage that occurs in *Katha* Upanishad about fools fancying themselves learned appears here with just one verbal change. Light is here thrown

* It should be remembered that the *Veda* was the encyclopaedia of all the knowledge of those days, and not a hymn-book only.

on what is meant by the important term *avidya* which occurs in the *Katha* and *Isavasya Upanishads* and also in the *Gita* (ch. 2, 42, 43).

I-(2)-7, 8

परीक्ष्य लोकान्कर्मचितान्ब्राह्मणो निर्वेदमायान्नास्त्यकृतः कृतेन ।
तद्विज्ञानार्थं स गुरुमेवाभिगच्छेत्समित्पाणिः श्रोत्रियं ब्रह्मनिष्ठम् ॥ १२ ॥

Realizing this, the seeker should abandon his desire and attachments for things transient, and respectfully approach a teacher who is qualified by learning and conduct to impart the higher knowledge.

I-(2)-12

तदेतत्सत्यम् यथा सुदीप्तात्पावकाद्विस्फुलिङ्गाः सहस्रशः प्रभवन्ते सरूपाः । तथाऽक्षराद्विविधाः सोम्य भावाः प्रजायन्ते तत्र चैवापि यन्ति ॥ १ ॥

This deals with the relationship between the Individual Soul and the Absolute Being.

The Soul is like the spark that is thrown out and re-absorbed by the blazing fire.

It is left to be inferred that it is of the same nature as the fire, and does not exist apart from it.

II-(1)-1

अग्निर्मूर्धा चक्षुषी चन्द्रसूर्यौ दिशः श्रोत्रे वाग्विवृताश्च वेदाः ।
वायुः प्राणो हृदयं विश्वमस्य पद्भ्यां पृथिवी ह्येष सर्वभूतान्तरात्मा ॥ ४ ॥
तस्मादग्निः समिधो यस्य सूर्यः सोमात्पर्जन्य ओषधयः पृथिव्याम् ।
पुमान् रेतः सिञ्चति योषितायां बह्वीः प्रजाः पुरुषात्संप्रसूताः ॥ ५ ॥

The whole universe is a manifestation and product of that universal, formless, causeless Being. The sun, moon and all the quarters, all knowledge, and the souls of all existing beings are parts and manifestations of that single all-immanent Being. All life and all qualities, functions and activities are forms of that single Energy. He is the Fire which has lighted the Sun and makes it burn, like a log burning in the fire. Thereby does the sun give us warmth and light. The rain does not rain, but it is He that rains through the clouds. Beings come together and multiply, but it is He alone that multiplies through them.

II-(1) 4. 5

अतः समुद्रा गिरयश्च सर्वेऽस्मात्स्यन्दन्ते सिन्धवः सर्वरूपाः । अतश्च
सर्वा ओषधयो रसाश्च येनैष भूतैस्तिष्ठते ह्यन्तरात्मा ॥ ९ ॥ पुरुष एवेदं
विश्वं कर्म तपो ब्रह्म परामृतम् । एतद्यो वेद निहितं गुहायां सोऽविद्याग्रन्थिं
विकिरतीह सोम्य ॥ १० ॥

From Him have issued all the mountains and the seas, the rivers, the trees and plants and their life-bearing essences. He who thus knows the Supreme Spirit that dwells within the heart, dear boy, cuts off all the knots of ignorance which bind man.

II-(1) 9-10

आविः संनिहितं गुहाचरं नाम महत्पदमत्रैतत्समर्पितम् । एजत्प्रा-
णन्निमिषच्च यदेतज्जानथ सदसद्वरेण्यं परं विज्ञानाद्यद्वरिष्ठं प्रजानाम् ॥ १ ॥

He has taken shape and dwells near, yea, in the cave of the human heart. Everything that moves, breathes or twinkles, moves and lives in Him. All that exists, as well as all ideas, even those which the mind indicates to itself as inconceivable, issue out of His presence.

II-(2) 1

धनुर्गृहीत्वौपनिषदं महास्त्रं शरं ह्युपासानिशितं संधयीत । आयम्य
तद्भावगतेन चेतसा लक्ष्यं तदेवाक्षरं सोम्य विद्धि ॥ ३ ॥ प्रणवो धनुः शरो
ह्यात्मा ब्रह्म तल्लक्ष्यमुच्यते । अप्रमत्तेन वेद्धव्यं शरवत्तन्मयो भवेत् ॥ ४ ॥

To perceive this Absolute Foundation of all existence, the mind must be as concentrated on it as an archer concentrates on his target. The Upanishad, i.e., knowledge received from the teacher, is the bow. The understanding Self should, like an arrow sharpened by devotion, be placed in it. Directing it at the target, *viz.*, the *Brahman,* pull the bow-string well with concentrated mind and you will hit the target. As a skilful archer, when aiming, makes his arrow merge in the target in his sight, and the two become but one and the same thing, so should your Self, the arrow, be merged by concentration in the target, *viz., Brahman.*

II-(2) 3, 4

When the pupil pulls the bow-string with steady aim, if the teacher asks him, "What do you see " the pupil should be able to reply truly that he sees nothing but the point he aims at. He must see neither bow, nor arrow, nor anything else but *Brahman*.

यस्मिन्द्यौः पृथिवी चान्तरिक्षमोतं मनः सह प्राणैश्च सर्वैः। तमेवैकं जानथ आत्मानमन्या वाचो विमुञ्चथामृतस्यैष सेतुः ॥५॥

He is the whole Universe. Heaven, Earth and Sky, your mind and your life-breath are all woven into Him. All other knowledge is a mere snare of words to be escaped from. He is the one and only Existence. This knowledge is the bridge leading to Immortality.

II-(2)-5

यः सर्वज्ञः सर्वविद्यस्यैष महिमा भुवि ॥ दिव्ये ब्रह्मपुरे ह्येष व्योम्न्यात्मा संप्रतिष्ठितः। मनोमयः प्राणशरीरनेता प्रतिष्ठितोऽन्ने हृदयं संनिधाय ॥ तद्विज्ञानेन परिपश्यन्ति धीरा आनन्दरूपममृतं यद्विभाति ॥ ६ ॥

He is within our own hearts. He has lodged Himself in the food-sustained body of men and rules both body and life, even He that sustains the whole universe and all its glory. The unruffled spirits contemplate on Him and realize his Deathless form of absolute joy.

II-(2)-7

भिद्यते हृदयग्रन्थिश्छिद्यन्ते सर्वसंशयाः। क्षीयन्ते चास्य कर्माणि तस्मिन्दृष्टे परावरे ॥ ८ ॥

When His presence in our own bodies and His immanence in every aspect of existence is realized, all doubts, all attachments and all activities vanish.

II-(2)-8

न तत्र सूर्यो भाति न चन्द्रतारकं नेमा विद्युतो भान्ति कुतोऽयमग्निः ।
तमेव भान्तमनुभाति सर्वं तस्य भासा सर्वमिदं विभाति ॥ १० ॥ ब्रह्मैवेद-
ममृतं पुरस्ताद्ब्रह्म पश्चाद्ब्रह्म दक्षिणतश्चोत्तरेण । अधश्चोर्ध्वं च प्रसृतं
ब्रह्मैवेदं विश्वमिदं वरिष्ठम् ॥ ११ ॥

On realizing Him, what is individual life? What even are the sun and the moon, the stars and the lightning of the clouds? What need be said, then, of this fire? All these are but reflections of that One Undying Light. He fills all the quarters and all overhead and down below. He alone exists.

II-(2)-10, 11

द्वा सुपर्णा सयुजा सखाया समानं वृक्षं परिषस्वजाते । तयोरन्यः
पिप्पलं स्वाद्वत्त्यनश्नन्नन्यो अभिचाकशीति ॥ १ ॥ समाने वृक्षे पुरुषो नि-
मग्नोऽनीशया शोचति मुह्यमानः । जुष्टं यदा पश्यत्यन्यमीशमस्य महिमान-
मिति वीतशोकः ॥ २ ॥ यदा पश्यः पश्यते रुक्मवर्णं कर्तारमीशं पुरुषं ब्रह्म-
योनिम् । तदा विद्वान् पुण्यपापे विधूय निरंजनः परमं साम्यमुपैति ॥ ३ ॥

Man's suffering lasts only until he sees the Supreme Being that dwells within himself. The Indwelling Supreme Spirit and the Individual Soul are like two birds. They cling to one another and are on the same tree. One eats the fruits of the tree, the other looks on, happy. One is attached to works, the other is free. When a man sees the Universal Ruler in himself, then the distinction between Good and Evil drops out. He is freed from passions and reaches the goal, i.e., becomes one with the Universal.

III-(1)-1, 3

How can one be enabled to have a vision of the Supreme Being within oneself? Mere learning does not reveal Him. One has to realize that the Lord is the life that lives and the light that shines in everything. When he realizes this, he loses his dependence on externals and finds bliss in himself.

प्राणो ह्येष यः सर्वभूतैर्विभाति विजानन्विद्वान्भवते नातिवादी।
आत्मक्रीड आत्मरतिः क्रियावानेष ब्रह्मविदां वरिष्ठः।

The man who realizes "It is the Supreme Life that shines in and through all life" does not waste words. His pleasures and his love are then all in the soul. He becomes the most enlightened among the philosophers.

III-(1)-4

सत्येन लभ्यस्तपसा ह्येष आत्मा सम्यग्ज्ञानेन ब्रह्मचर्येण नित्यम्।
अन्तःशरीरे ज्योतिर्मयो हि शुभ्रो यं पश्यन्ति यतयः क्षीणदोषाः ॥

Truth, penance, understanding and purity are essential requisites for this revelation of the *Brahman* within. When the heart is cleansed, *Brahman* is revealed, and He is seen shining like a burning light within oneself.

III-(1)-5

सत्यमेव जयते नानृतं सत्येन पन्था विततो देवयानः। येनाक्रम-
न्त्यृषयो ह्याप्तकामा यत्र तत्सत्यस्य परमं निधानम् ॥

Truth wins ever, and not untruth. With Truth is paved the road to the Divine. On that road walk the *Rishis* with desires all quenched to reach the Supreme Abode of Truth.

III-(1)-6

Truth is the only pathway to God, and the seers pursue this to reach Him. This emphatic dependence on Truth is the dominating characteristic of the Upanishads.

The Lord is not to be apprehended by the senses, but only by the mind into which all the senses have been drawn in. All thought is interwoven with the senses, and it is only when the mind is released from all this and is in a state of perfect freedom and tranquillity, that the Lord reveals Himself.

न चक्षुषा गृह्यते नापि वाचा नान्यैर्देवैस्तपसा कर्मणा वा। ज्ञान-
प्रसादेन विशुद्धसत्त्वस्ततस्तु तं पश्यते निष्कलं ध्यायमानः ॥ ८ ॥ एषोऽणु-
रात्मा चेतसा वेदितव्यो यस्मिन्प्राणः पंचधा संविवेश। प्राणैश्चित्तं सर्वमोतं
प्रजानां यस्मिन्विशुद्धे विभवत्येष आत्मा ॥ ९ ॥

Not by the eyes nor by speech or through other senses can He be apprehended: not even by austerities or ceremonials. He whose mind is pure and serene can by meditation attain a vision of the Indivisible. The Subtle Spirit dwelling within, into which the fivefold life has entered, can be realized by the understanding. If the understanding that is pierced and pervaded by the senses is purified, then the spirit reveals itself unto it.

III-(1)-8. 9

नायमात्मा प्रवचनेन लभ्यो न मेधया न बहुना श्रुतेन। यमेवैष वृणुते तेन लभ्यस्तस्यैष आत्मा विवृणुते तनुं स्वाम् ॥

This appears in the *Kathopanishad* also.

Much learning or scholarly discussion, or force of intellect cannot enable one to realize the Spirit within.

The Spirit that yearns for self-realization realizes itself.

III-(2)-3

The yearning for realization automatically destroys other desires and attachments, and enables one to reach self-realization.

The feeble-minded, who do not make earnest effort through well-directed meditation and control of mind and senses, cannot hope to realize the Self within. The will to realize and strenuous effort are necessary. *Balam* in the following *sloka* stands for effort and strength exercised in the way of self-control and steady application.

नायमात्मा बलहीनेन लभ्यो न च प्रमादात्तपसो वाप्यलिङ्गात् ।
एतैरुपायैर्यतते यस्तु विद्वांस्तस्यैष आत्मा विशते ब्रह्मधाम ॥

Realization of the Soul cannot be attained by a man who has not strength and a vigilant spirit. It cannot be attained by austerities without devotion.

But if with undertanding a man strives with these aids, his soul enters the Abode of *Brahman*.

III-(2)-4

वेदान्तविज्ञानसुनिश्चितार्थाः संन्यासयोगाद्यतयः शुद्धसत्त्वाः । ते ब्रह्मलोकेषु परान्तकाले परामृताः परिमुच्यन्ति सर्वे ॥ ६ ॥

यथा नद्यः स्यन्दमानाः समुद्रेऽस्तं गच्छन्ति नामरूपे विहाय । तथा विद्वान्नामरूपाद्विमुक्तः परात्परं पुरुषमुपैति दिव्यम् ॥ ८ ॥

Knowledge and discipline are mutually complementary. *Vedanta* explains the true nature of what we seek. *Yoga,* i.e., detachment and self-discipline, purifies the mind and enables it to perceive the Truth. Those whose understanding has been thus enlightened as well as purified become one with the Universal Spirit. They join the Supreme Being and lose themselves in Him even as all the rivers join and lose themselves in the great ocean.

II-(2)-6, 8

Here ends our little book. Let us bow to the Rishis.

नमः परम ऋषिभ्योः । नमः परम ऋषिभ्यः ।

INDEX OF SLOKAS QUOTED